GU00836312

HOW OLD IS E

W.G. Hoskins at the White Hart Hotel, South Street, Exeter,
in the final scene of the last programme of his television
series *Landscapes of England* (BBC2, 14 June 1978).

© Getty Images, reproduced by permission.

HOW OLD IS EXETER?

Divining the Distant Past with W.G. Hoskins

T.P. Wiseman

THE
MINT
PRESS

The Mint Press 2016

© The Mint Press

ISBN 978-1-903356-66-1

No part of this publication may be reproduced, stored in a
retrieval system or transmitted in any form or by any means, electronic,
mechanical, photocopying, recording or otherwise, without
the prior permission of the copyright holders.

Cover designed by Topics – The Creative Partnership, Exeter

Typeset by Kestrel Data, Exeter

Printed and bound in Great Britain by Short Run Press Ltd, Exeter

Contents

Illustrations

1

The Lesson of Honeychurch

W.G. Hoskins' magnificent history of Devon was published sixty years ago (1954). It's a great work, and what makes it so is not only the immense amount of detailed information it contains, but also the extraordinary grace and clarity of the author's style. Let's begin with an extended example of what I mean by that.

It comes in the chapter on ecclesiastical history. After a brief description of the diocese of Exeter and its parochial structure, which he describes as 'the mere mechanics of religious life', this is what he writes:[1]

> How can we penetrate to the reality of the spiritual life of the medieval centuries, to the unrecorded attitudes and thoughts of unlettered peasants, of their almost equally unlettered parsons, or even of the monastic houses wrapped in contemplation among the green woods and valleys of medieval Devon? . . .
>
> Perhaps we get nearest to the heart of the matter when we walk alone in the lanes of a remote parish like Honeychurch, and penetrate at length to the little church that stands beside an even quieter lane, with its rubble masonry from a local quarry softened by lichens to half-tones of grey and green, and

[1] WGH, *Devon* (London 1954 = Andover 2003) 226-7.

its dumpy western tower housing the original three medieval bells, now silent. . . . We push open the heavy door, and with it the centuries roll back: this withdrawn Norman church on the site of one even older, small and aisleless, only a plain nave and chancel: there was never any need to enlarge the church at Honeychurch. There, at the back under the curtained tower arch, is the mutilated font of Bishop Bartholomew's time, crowned unevenly by a worn, slightly comic, cover of Jacobean date; here are the leaning wormy benches of rustic carpentry – some 15th-century carpenter from Sampford Courtenay no doubt made them – the pulpit from which the doctrines of the Elizabethan Church were the first to be heard, the curtains, the plastered and bossed roof, the plain granite chancel arch.

It is all so worn and uneven, not a straight line anywhere, soaked with so many centuries of the Latin Mass spoken to a small gathering of Devonshire farmers and labourers and their households. In the light from the clear glass of the windows, we almost hear again the mumbled Litanies and Collects on 18th-century Sunday mornings, the murmur of the Lord's Prayer and the Psalms spoken in broad Devonshire voices, the immemorial words of the English Sunday they knew by heart. The buzz of flies in the sunlit windows, and the subdued farmyard sounds coming through the open doorway, the smell of the churchyard grasses, take us back immediately to those placid days when men and women worshipped in the midst of their work and their homes, among their numerous children and beside the graves of their ancestors. For a few moments we feel a little of the things that moved them inwardly year after year at the appointed times.

It is a beautifully evocative passage – but it's not just fine writing for the reader's pleasure. It's also a historian's attempt to reach something for which no documentary evidence ever existed, 'the *unrecorded* attitudes and thoughts of *unlettered* peasants'. And

2000	Here and now
1900	*Devon* published 1954
1800	
1700	
1600	
1500	English Reformation
1400	
1300	Black Death 1348
1200	
1100	
1000	Norman conquest 1066
900	
800	
700	
600	Saxon conquest
500	
400	End of Roman rule
300	
200	
100	
BC/AD	Roman conquest AD 43
100	
200	

Fig. 1.   Time-chart for the history of Exeter, marking
cultural discontinuities

he knows the point beyond which it can't be done. Only the Anglican liturgy, 'the immemorial words of the English Sunday', can offer him the illusion of inhabiting their world. This is how he goes on:

Even so, it is difficult to think back beyond the barrier of the Reformation, that great wall between us and the medieval past. If at times we can feel imaginatively a kinship with the English men and women worshipping in their plain Protestant churches in Stuart and Georgian times, we can feel no imaginative link with those who went before them, except a faint pulse now and then. Four hundred years of Anglican religion have moulded and coloured the historian's mind also, and he finds it difficult to apprehend the inner life of pre-Reformation men and women, however linked he may be to the places where they lived.

That 'barrier' of the Reformation, the wall that keeps us out of the thought-world of the Middle Ages, is a very powerful image. How can the historian ever describe what lies behind it?

Chronology is always hard to visualise. To understand the passage of time properly, we need to see it to scale. So I offer a time chart [Fig. 1], reading down century by century from the here and now. What we have to bear in mind is that each and every one of those centuries is itself a period much longer than living memory. Yes, of course people listen to what their grandparents tell them, but even so, without written documentation the past is lost within three generations.

I have marked only the most hugely significant events in that *longue durée*, the cultural discontinuities when people's lives were profoundly and irreversibly disrupted. If the Reformation is indeed 'that great wall between us and the medieval past', then how much *more* impenetrable to us must be the experience of what happened in Devon two thousand years ago, behind a whole long sequence of such 'barriers' to the transmission of memory and understanding?

2

Hoskins on Exeter

Hoskins was born in 1908 in Exeter, at the house on St David's Hill where the commemorative blue plaque quotes the Virgilian epigraph he used for the *Devon* volume: *hic amor, haec patria est*, 'this is my love, this my native land'.[2] He left it in 1930, and from 1931 to 1941 he lived and worked in Leicester, teaching Economics and Commerce at the University College there; after war service as a statistician in London, he returned to Leicester in 1946 and ran the newly-founded Department of Local History from 1948 to 1951, when he was appointed to a Readership in Economic History at the University of Oxford.[3]

The post involved no college teaching, and Hoskins and his family lived fourteen miles out of town at Steeple Barton. As his obituarist puts it, 'the Oxford years between 1951 and 1965 gave Hoskins all the time he sought to complete books long maturing in his head.' The two principal ones were the Devon history,

[2] Virgil *Aeneid* 4.347 (Aeneas telling Dido about Latium); *Devon* (n. 1 above) xxi = xxxvii. Hoskins used it again (misattributing it to Horace) in *One Man's England* (London 1978) 132.
[3] Details in Joan Thirsk, 'William George Hoskins 1908–1992', *Proceedings of the British Academy* 87 (1995) 338-54.

commissioned in 1947, and *The Making of the English Landscape*, first planned in 1949.[4] *Devon* went to press in the autumn of 1952, and the introduction is dated 9 January 1953;[5] *The Making of the English Landscape* was written between July 1953 and the end of January 1954.[6] As soon as the second book was published, in 1955, Hoskins moved from Steeple Barton to his home town of Exeter, and for the next ten years commuted to Oxford only in term-time.[7]

Hoskins always loved Exeter, but I think there was a more specific reason for this relocation. In the Devon history, he explained at three separate places that the city of Exeter deserved separate treatment, and would receive it in a forthcoming volume of the same series.[8] Or more than one: 'There is no adequate history of Exeter,' he wrote in 1960, 'and to write one would be a life-work and fill two or three substantial volumes.' That was exactly what he hoped to do himself, but alas, it never came about: as he acknowledged sadly in 1969, 'the large history of my native city which I had hoped to write will never be done now'.[9] But it does seem clear that in 1955 he was intending to get on with it straight away, and wanted to be based in the city to do it.

If that's right, then it is reasonable to assume that he would first turn his mind to the origins of Exeter – and it so happens that we can detect, at precisely that time, a radical shift in his opinion on the subject.

[4] Thirsk (n. 3 above) 346, 349 (quotation), 350.
[5] *Devon* (n. 1 above) xix-xx = xxxiv-xxxv.
[6] Thirsk (n. 3 above) 349.
[7] And to Leicester from 1965 to 1968: see Thirsk (n. 3 above) 351 for his tenure of the Hatton Professorship of English Local History.
[8] *Devon* (n. 1 above) vi, xviii = xxxii-iii, 393; the series was 'A New Survey of England', of which only Hoskins' *Devon* and Michael Robbins' *Middlesex* ever appeared (Peter Beacham in *Devon* [2003 edition] xviii-xix).
[9] WGH, *Two Thousand Years in Exeter* (Exeter 1960) v, (Chichester 1969) vi.

In the nineteenth century, historians had assumed without argument that the Roman city of Isca Dumnoniorum was built on the site of some pre-existing hill-fort or *oppidum*.[10] There was no positive evidence for that, and as it turned out, it was the disastrous history of the twentieth century that enabled the idea to be empirically tested. In April and May 1942, Exeter was blitzed, with incendiaries and high explosives, and about half the historic city centre was laid waste. Even before the war was over, a committee was set up to conduct archaeological excavations in the devastated city centre, and Aileen Fox – that is, Lady Fox, wife of Sir Cyril – was appointed as Director.[11]

One of the questions she wanted to address was whether there had indeed been a pre-Roman Exeter,[12] and the answer she came up with was clearly negative. 'It has often been suggested,' she wrote in her final report, 'that Exeter may have begun as an Early Iron Age settlement, but the evidence from the 1945–7 excavations is against this. Every early stratum, resting directly on the natural soil or old turf layer, contained Roman pottery, and other objects. No hand-made Iron Age B sherds were found.'[13] Archaeology had established a new consensus, and naturally Hoskins followed it.

---

[10] e.g. Rev. George Oliver, *The History of the City of Exeter* (Exeter and London 1861) 1; R.N. Worth, 'Presidential Address: Roman Devon', *Transactions of the Devonshire Association* 23 (1891) 25-101, at 51-2; Edward A. Freeman, 'The Place of Exeter in the History of England', *Archaeological Journal* 30 (1873) 297-318, at 302-6; idem, *Exeter* (London 1887) 5-6; J.C. Wall, in *The Victoria History of the County of Devon* vol. 1 (London 1906) 606.

[11] Aileen Fox, *Roman Exeter: Excavations in the War-Damaged Areas 1945–1947* (Manchester 1952).

[12] Aileen Fox, *Aileen: A Pioneering Archaeologist* (Leominster 2000) 104: one of the 'problems which I had to try to solve [was] . . . the origins of the Roman city, whether it started as an Iron Age settlement'.

[13] Fox (n. 11 above) 14.

In 1952, the same year the report on the excavations came out, Hoskins published an attractive booklet entitled *Old Exeter*, in which his account of the origin of the city was explicitly based on the new evidence:[14]

> Archaeologists have long sought for evidence of a pre-Roman origin for Exeter, in view of its early appearance as a tribal capital – *Isca Dumnoniorum*. Recent excavations in the bomb-damaged areas, and the evidence of coins found over the last century or more, show fairly conclusively, however, that the site was first selected by the Romans about the middle of the first century. We can now say with some confidence that the Romans built upon this hill about A.D. 50 and that the site of Exeter is unlikely to have been occupied before then.

That was the line he took also in the history of Devon:[15]

> The Romans halted their advance on the Exe: beyond lay the Celtic West into which they did not bother to penetrate. And here, on a steep-sided ridge rising a hundred feet above the river-frontier, they founded about A.D. 50 the town of *Isca*, which took its name from the river. Isca became the tribal capital of the Dumnonii, the people who occupied Devon and Cornwall, and at *Isca Dumnoniorum* their kings must have reigned for centuries.

Hoskins was very conscious that he was no expert on this period, and in the Introduction to the Devon history he expressed his

[14] WGH, *Old Exeter: A Description of its Growth and Old Buildings* (London 1952) 4-5.
[15] *Devon* (n. 1 above) 393-4; presupposed also at 34-5, 36 ('founded in the reign of Nero'), 38 ('founded late in the reign of Claudius').

regret that he had not been able to consult Sir Cyril and Lady Fox as much as he would have liked.[16]

Of course no-one then knew that Roman Exeter was at first a legionary fortress, and that the town of Isca Dumnoniorum didn't exist before about AD 80; that was only discovered in 1971, with the excavation of the legionary bath-house in the cathedral close. But in 1954 Hoskins had got the essentials right: Roman occupation did indeed begin about AD 50, soon after Claudius' invasion, and there was no reason to think there was any hill fort or tribal centre previously existing on the site. He even found an opportunity to repeat the point in *The Making of the English Landscape*:[17]

> The Romans founded many new towns during the second half of the first century and the early part of the second century, mostly on virgin sites, as at Exeter (Isca Dumnoniorum), which was founded about A.D. 50.

That was his firm opinion, clearly stated, explicitly based on the latest archaeological evidence, at the time he moved to Exeter in 1955. But it didn't take him long to change his mind.

One of Hoskins' early projects, on taking up permanent residence in Exeter, was to produce, for schools and the general public, 'potted' versions of both the Devon history he had just completed and the Exeter history to which he was now addressing himself. *Devon and its People* appeared in 1959, and *Two Thousand Years in Exeter* in 1960; both books were published in the first instance by local firms, the Devon book by Wheaton's, the Exeter one by James Townsend.

---

[16] *Devon* (n. 1 above) xvii = xxxii; also 572 = 577 for acknowledgements to Ralegh Radford and Aileen Fox ('neither is responsible for any errors').
[17] WGH, *The Making of the English Landscape* (London 1955) 34 = (Harmondsworth 1970) 40.

The first chapter of *Devon and its People*, 'Prehistoric Devon', concludes with a section on Iron Age agriculture and trade:[18]

> At Topsham on the estuary of the river Exe we have also found some traces of a prehistoric trading settlement, and it is very likely that Exeter, too, was an important settlement, with some traders, two hundred years before the Romans took it over.

Really? Where did that idea come from? What was his evidence for this 'trading settlement', if the excavations had found no trace of it?

If we turn to *Two Thousand Years in Exeter*, published the following year, we find the answer on the first page:

> There is good reason to believe that the site of Exeter, or part of it, was occupied some considerable time before the Romans appeared on the scene. This takes us back to a time well before written records, and we depend therefore on certain material evidence for our scanty knowledge of this distant time. This material evidence is mainly that of coins which have been found within the city during various kinds of excavations in the past 150 years; and there is also the evidence of ancient tradition.

So it seems that Hoskins had two reasons for changing his mind about how old Exeter is – some coins, and a mysterious 'ancient tradition'. Let's take them in that order, the coins first.

---

[18] WGH, *Devon and its People* (Exeter 1959 = Newton Abbot 1968) 18.

3

Captain Shortt's Evidence

The story of the coins is quite a long one, and it's supposed to have begun in 1810, when Exeter was reconstructing itself as a modern city and a new main sewer was being laid below High Street and Fore Street. In the stretch between Broadgate and Milk Street (say fifty yards either side of the Carfax), at a depth of about twenty feet, it was said that nearly a thousand Greek coins were found, their dates ranging from the early third century BC to the eleventh century AD. When the medieval Broadgate itself was demolished in 1823, the works supposedly revealed another 120 Greek coins with a similar range of dates.

These collections were first documented in 1841 by Captain W.T.P. Shortt, an enthusiastic antiquarian who had come to live in Exeter nine years earlier. He had not been an eye-witness of the finds, but he was able to examine and identify the coins that were still available.[19] He innocently assumed they were evidence of very long-lasting trade links with the eastern Mediterranean, but he was baffled by the question of how they

---

[19] W.T.P. Shortt, *Sylva Antiqua Iscana, Numismatica, quinetiam Figulina, or Roman and Other Antiquities of Exeter* (Exeter and London n.d.) 90-102. The publication is dated to March 1841 by R.G. Goodchild, 'An Antiquary of Devon (W.T.P. Shortt, 1800–1881)', *Transactions of the Devonshire Association* 79 (1947) 229-55.

were all accumulated in the place where they were found.[20]

The obvious explanation was offered in 1907 by two professional historians, F.J. Haverfield and Sir George MacDonald. Their assessment of Shortt's material was briskly dismissive:[21]

We are dealing here with some modern collection of Eastern Mediterranean coins, and not with the results of ancient trade. No other conjecture will explain the occurrence, at a place like Exeter, of issues belonging to the same regions, and yet extending over fifteen centuries.

Haverfield and MacDonald concluded that Shortt had been duped, and the coins had not originated from the deep levels of Exeter at all.[22]

That damning verdict held the field for thirty years. But in 1937 it was challenged by Richard Goodchild and J.G. Milne, who claimed that other Greek coins turning up in Exeter had confirmed the authenticity of Shortt's material.[23] In 1947, Goodchild's study of Shortt's Exeter career repeated his conviction that the antiquary had *not* been duped,[24] and the following year Milne used the alleged Exeter finds to illustrate a more general hypothesis, that Hellenistic bronze coins were

---

[20] Shortt (n. 19 above) 90: 'Cleverer heads than ours would be puzzled to tell by what magic they all got crammed 20 feet underground into this subterrene Babylonish spot . . .'

[21] F.J. Haverfield and G. MacDonald, 'Greek Coins at Exeter', *Numismatic Chronicle* 4.7 (1907) 145-55.

[22] [F.J.] Haverfield, 'Isca Dumnoniorum', *Paulys Realencyclopädie der classischen Altertumswissenschaft* 9 (1916) 2056-7: 'Die dort im Anfang des 19. Jhdts. reichlich gefundenen griechischen Münzen stammen nicht von der Römerzeit, sondern von modernen Schwindlern.'

[23] R.G. Goodchild and J.G. Milne, 'The Greek Coins from Exeter Reconsidered', *Numismatic Chronicle* 5.17 (1937) 124-34.

[24] Goodchild (n. 19 above) 238.

widely imported into southern Britain for use as bullion.[25]

That was how things stood in the late fifties, when Hoskins began work on his big history of the city, and wrote *Two Thousand Years in Exeter* as a popular forerunner to it. It is easy to see why he started with the coin evidence, but his treatment of it was a little disingenuous. This is how he put it:[26]

> In the year 1810, a considerable number of Hellenistic coins – that is, coins of ancient Greek types from the eastern Mediterranean – were found in Broadgate, while workmen were digging at a depth of twenty feet. These coins, the largest discovery of their kind yet made in this country, could be dated as belonging to the third, second, and first centuries before Christ. They suggested some sort of trade at Exeter with the Mediterranean countries some time between say 250 B.C. and the birth of Christ.

In fact, the vast majority of those thousand or so Greek coins were from the Roman period; only about 35 were Hellenistic.[27] One might just as well pick on the fifteen Byzantine examples, and make a case for 'trade at Exeter with the Mediterranean countries' in the sixth and seventh centuries AD – the very time, in fact, when Hoskins in a later chapter noted the absence of coins as indicating the absence of trade.[28]

Very properly, Hoskins alluded to the scepticism of Haverfield and MacDonald; but he also noted the counter-arguments of Goodchild and Milne in defence of Shortt's material, and he took it for granted that the result was decisive in their favour:[29]

[25] J.G. Milne, *Finds of Greek Coins in the British Isles* (London 1948) 25-9.
[26] WGH, *Two Thousand Years in Exeter* (Exeter 1960 = Chichester 2004) 1.
[27] See the list at Haverfield and MacDonald (n. 21 above) 151-3.
[28] *Two Thousand Years* (n. 26 above) 11 = 14, on the fifth and sixth centuries AD.
[29] *Two Thousand Years* (n. 26 above) 2 = 1-2.

We must, therefore, accept the conclusion that there was considerable trading between the Mediterranean countries and southern Britain a century or two before the birth of Christ, and that Exeter (under some other name) was one of the places engaged in this trade. . . . Roughly speaking, then, we may say that there were people living in Exeter about 200 years or more before the Romans came, and that Exeter as an inhabited place is about 2,100 years old.

That was enough to justify the challenging title of his book: the Roman foundation that the archaeologists insisted on, and that he himself had previously accepted, would take Exeter back only 1900 years before the date of publication.

Even on its own terms, Hoskins' argument was not as cogent as he thought. The presence of Hellenistic coins might indicate trade, but it didn't prove Exeter was an early trading centre. Goodchild himself, who insisted so strongly on the genuineness of the coin finds, did not believe in a pre-Roman town. He knew that bronze coins could remain in circulation for centuries, so those Hellenistic coins weren't necessarily newly minted.[30] But Hoskins ignored all that. For him, the coins proved the existence

---

[30] R.G. Goodchild, *Roman Exeter (The City of Isca Dumnoniorum): A Summary* (Exeter 1946) 5-6: 'Despite the geographical features which made Exeter so suitable a site for prehistoric occupation, there is virtually no evidence that it did in fact have a pre-Roman population . . . [P]re-Roman Exeter must remain in the realms of legend rather than among accepted facts.' Goodchild and Milne (n. 23 above) 127: 'To accept as authentic the Exeter Greek coins does not necessarily entail trespassing on the dangerous ground of pre-Roman archaeology. Scanty as the evidence is, it suggests that even the earliest Greek coins could have been deposited in Roman times; such deposit, although uncommon, is certainly not unparalleled.' Also Goodchild (above) 6: 'If [the Greek coins] reached Exeter in antiquity, it was probably during the Roman period.'

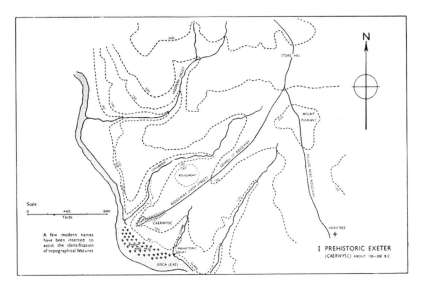

Fig. 2.   Plan of 'Caerwysc' from Hoskins' *Two Thousand Years in Exeter*

of a pre-Roman trading centre – and he was even prepared to
make a plan of it [Fig. 2].[31]

He called his conjectured town 'Caerwysc', which is
what Asser, the biographer of King Alfred, writing of a
time a thousand years later, gave as the Welsh equivalent of
the Saxon 'Exanceastre'.[32] Its main features, he thought,
were two 'ridgeway' routes, one along the line of Polsloe
Road to Heavitree, and the main one along the line of Old
Tiverton Road, Sidwell Street and High Street. The latter,
he confidently announced, 'must have been the main route
of those early traders. It is significant that the biggest finds

---

[31] *Two Thousand Years* (n. 26 above) 6/7 map I = 2 fig. 1.
[32] Asserius *De rebus gestis Aelfredi* 49 (referring to the year 876): *locum qui dicitur
Saxonice Exanceastre, Britannice autem Caeruuisc.*

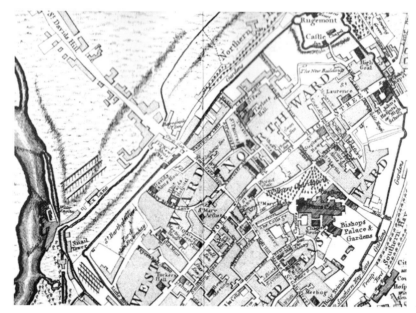

Fig. 3.   Part of Benjamin Donn's 1765 plan of Exeter,
showing 'Little Britain' (bottom left)

of ancient coins were made within a few yards of the High
Street.'[33]

So where were they coming from, these traders, dropping
their coins along the way? Hoskins wasn't sure: 'The ridgeway
came down over Stoke Hill (from where, we do not yet know)'.[34]
But he was quite sure he knew where they were heading. On his
plan, the route ends at a place marked 'camp', evidently used
in the old sense of the word to mean a hill-fort. In *Devon and
its People*, Hoskins had referred to 'the great hilltop fortresses or

---

[33] *Two Thousand Years* (n. 26 above) 3.
[34] *Two Thousand Years* (n. 26 above) 2 = 3.

16

"camps" that we see to-day all over Devon',[35] and that was what he meant here too:[36]

> The ridge along which the High Street ran ended in a spur overlooking the river. The tip of this spur is what is now the disused churchyard of Allhallows-on-the-Walls, ending at the turn of the city walls known as Snail's Tower [Fig. 3]. On this spur the British had an earthwork – a hill-fortress – of the same type as those we see on the hill-tops of Hembury or Woodbury, though not so grand or formidable. This was their fortress in times of emergency.

Well, of course it is *possible* that there was once a small promontory hill-fort at that point, just as it is *possible* that there were once trade routes along those ridges. It's just that in neither case is there any positive reason to think so.

In Hoskins' view, the main habitation area – 'hardly more than a native village, despite its widespread trading activities' – was between Bartholomew Street and Fore Street. He had a very particular reason for believing that, and it is worth dwelling on it for a moment as an indication of how he felt able to read the distant past. This is how the paragraph just quoted continues:

> It seems probable that the earliest inhabitants lived in huts on the leeward side of this spur, on ground sloping gently down to the riverside. Centuries later, this part of Exeter was still known

---

[35] *Devon and its People* (n. 18 above) 16; *Oxford English Dictionary* s.v. 'camp' I.1 ('as used of ancient works, Roman, British, Danish, etc., it usually means the intrenched and fortified site, within which an army lodged or defended itself').

[36] *Two Thousand Years* (n. 26 above) 3.

as Britayne (before its name was changed to Bartholomew Street) for it preserved the memory of the time when the ancient British lived there.

That is offered not as a hypothesis but as a fact. How Hoskins thought he knew it becomes clear when he repeats the point in the next chapter, relating king Athelstan's expulsion of the *Britones* still living in *Execestra* in about 928:[37]

> There can be little doubt that the British quarter between 658 and 928 lay in the original area of ancient British settlement, in the district roughly marked by Bartholomew Street today. For centuries during the Middle Ages this street was known as Britayne, a reference to the memory that it was once the British quarter.

I think one is entitled to ask whose memory could possibly have reached back from the Middle Ages to a time two hundred years before the Roman conquest.

The toponym 'Britayne' for Bartholomew Street is first attested in a document of about 1250; on Hooker's map of 1587, and others subsequently [Fig. 3], it is given as 'Little Britaine'.[38] The learned authors of *The Place-Names of Devon* make the entirely reasonable suggestion that 'this street, like Little Britain in London (*Brettone street* 1329, *Pety Bryttayne* 1561), may owe its name to a settlement of Bretons'. Given the constant close relations between Brittany and south-west England, of which of course

---

[37] *Two Thousand Years* (n. 26 above) 12 = 14; William of Malmesbury *Gesta regum Anglorum* 2.134.6.

[38] J.E.B. Gover, A. Mawer and F.M. Stenton, *The Place-Names of Devon* (English Place-Name Society vol. VIII, Cambridge 1931) 21; Todd Gray, *Exeter Maps* (Exeter 2006) 9-11, 13, 18, 20-23.

Hoskins was well aware,[39] there's no reason to look for any other explanation. If the name were a historical puzzle with no other possible solution, one might be prepared to entertain Hoskins' far-fetched idea. But it isn't; the solution is obvious, and there is no need to try to believe that the Britons of the pre-Roman world were part of Exeter's memory fourteen centuries later.

All these arguments, good or bad as they may be, are predicated on a single assumption, that the Greek coins catalogued by Captain Shortt really were found twenty feet down in the soil of Exeter in 1810 and 1823. That was what enabled Hoskins to believe in a pre-Roman town trading with the Mediterranean. At the time he was writing, the latest contributions to the controversy were by Goodchild and Milne, who believed in the authenticity of Shortt's material. It was only in 1991, a few months before his death, that expert opinion shifted decisively in the other direction.

When the Exeter Museums Archaeological Field Unit set about publishing the finds from the excavations of 1971–79, the opportunity was taken to re-examine the Greek coins listed by Shortt, some of which had been preserved in the Royal Albert Memorial Museum ever since 1881.[40] The task was entrusted to George Boon of the National Museum of Wales, a distinguished numismatist who was also a very experienced archaeological excavator. It was immediately clear to him that the collection showed no sign of the patination and extensive corrosion that would be expected of coins recovered from centuries buried in the earth; he also pointed out that the distribution of types was

[39] *Devon* (n. 1 above) 200: 'There were continual contacts between Brittany and south-western Britain from prehistoric times onwards, across the hundred miles of open water.'

[40] George C. Boon, 'Byzantine and other exotic ancient bronze coins from Exeter', in Neil Holbrook and Paul T. Bidwell (eds), *Roman Finds from Exeter* (Exeter Archaeological Reports vol. 4, Exeter 1991) 38-45.

characteristic of nineteenth-century coin collections brought back from the eastern Mediterranean by service personnel and other travellers.

So it is pointless to try to make historical sense of that paradoxical sequence of coins from Hellenistic to Byzantine. The stories Shortt was told about the great discoveries of 1810 and 1823 were evidently untrue.[41] And that means that the main premise of Hoskins' narrative of pre-Roman Exeter was invalid. All that was left was 'the evidence of ancient tradition' – and to that we must now turn.

[41] The alleged finds 'are shown to be spurious' (Holbrook and Bidwell [n. 40 above] back cover).

4

'Ancient Tradition'

The second chapter of *Devon and its People* is entitled 'Devon in Roman Times'. It contains the following paragraph:[42]

> There is an ancient tradition that the Roman general Vespasian, who commanded the Second Legion, besieged the *oppidum* or fortress at Exeter for eight days in 49 A.D. It is also said that a British king marched rapidly from the east of the country and fought with Vespasian just outside Exeter. Each army suffered severely and neither gained a victory, but in the morning peace was made and the *Dumnonii* seem to have given the Romans no further trouble.

'It is quite likely,' he goes on, 'that this ancient tradition is true.'

So too the following year, in *Two Thousand Years in Exeter*, Hoskins attributed to 'ancient tradition' a story that Vespasian besieged the place that was later Exeter:[43]

---

[42] *Devon and its People* (n. 18 above) 19-20; in the third sentence the text has 'seemed to have given', which I assume was not what Hoskins meant.
[43] *Two Thousand Years* (n. 26 above) 6 = 5.

The tradition tells us that there was already a settlement here when Vespasian was sent westwards, and so supplements the evidence of the Hellenistic coins. At the time of this siege Exeter is said to have been called by the rather formidable name of Caer-pen-huel-goit, which means 'the fortified town on the hill near the high or great wood'.

Other scholars translate the name differently,[44] but that's not the problem. The problem is that we already know the Celtic name for Exeter: it was Caeruuisc, as reported by Asser, king Alfred's biographer, in about 893, and as used by Hoskins in his own reconstruction of the pre-Roman site. When he now tells us that 'an even older name occurs in the tradition', I think we may reasonably wonder why it should have been remembered, and how it could have been transmitted.

Hoskins was a scrupulous historian, and of course he knew his position had to be defended. This is how he proceeded:[45]

The tradition of a siege by Vespasian has generally been discredited by modern historians, mainly on the ground that it appears in the writings of a chronicler (Geoffrey of Monmouth) who is known to be very inaccurate, if no worse. He tells us that Vespasian was sent down by the Emperor Claudius to subdue South-West Britain, and that he besieged Exeter for eight days without success. A British king then arrived from the east with an army and fought with Vespasian. Despite great losses on both sides neither got the victory. The next morning, by the mediation of the British queen, the two leaders made peace.

---

[44] e.g. 'the town at the head of the mine in the wood': J.S.P. Tatlock, *The Legendary History of Britain: Geoffrey of Monmouth's* Historia Regum Britanniae *and its Early Vernacular Versions* (Berkeley and Los Angeles 1950) 50-1.
[45] *Two Thousand Years* (n. 26 above) 6-7 = 6.

So now we have the source of the information, and we'll come to Geoffrey of Monmouth in a moment. What I want us to notice first is Hoskins' repeated use of that talismanic phrase 'an ancient tradition'.

Let's just remind ourselves of the chronology [Fig. 1]. Remember the passage we began with, where Hoskins found it impossible to think himself back beyond 'the barrier of the Reformation'. Now, just five years later, he was offering a detailed narrative of the defence of a pre-Roman hill-fort in the first century AD. Just look again at the time chart, with all those historical turning points, those irreversible dislocations of the structure of society. What sort of 'tradition' could possibly have survived them all, to provide us with a *true* story?

We do, of course, have an accurate narrative of the Roman invasion itself. The surviving texts of well-informed classical authors – Tacitus, Suetonius, Dio Cassius – tell us about the initial advance to the Thames and the capture of the British capital at Camulodunum (Colchester); and because the military career of a future emperor was of interest, they also tell us something of the part played by Vespasian as one of the legionary commanders.[46] But they don't tell us much:[47]

Claudio principe Narcissi gratia legatus legionis in Germaniam missus est; inde in Britanniam translatus tricies cum hoste conflixit. Duas ualidissimas gentes superque uiginti oppida et insulam Vectem Britanniae proximam in dicionem redegit.

When Claudius was emperor, Vespasian was sent to Germany as a legionary commander thanks to the influence of Narcissus [one of Claudius' powerful freedmen]; from there he was

---

[46] Tacitus *Agricola* 13.3; Suetonius *Diuus Claudius* 17, *Diuus Vespasianus* 4.1; Dio Cassius 60.19-23. Vespasian's legion is named as the Second Augusta in Tacitus *Histories* 3.44.1.

[47] Suetonius *Diuus Vespasianus* 4.1.

transferred to Britain, where he fought thirty engagements with the enemy. He brought into subjection two very strong peoples, more than twenty hill-forts, and the island of Wight, which lies close to Britain.

And that's it. How far west Vespasian got during his time in command, and whether the Dumnonii were one of those 'very strong peoples', the classical authors don't tell us. Archaeology, in the form of Mortimer Wheeler's spectacular excavations at Maiden Castle,[48] has enabled us to identify one of those peoples as the Durotriges of Dorset; but that's as far as real history can take us.

Hoskins did his best to link the story of Vespasian's siege of Exeter with the authentic narrative. 'There is,' he says,[49] 'good independent evidence to support this ancient tradition' – namely the attested presence of the Second Legion at Seaton in East Devon,[50] and the coins of the emperor Claudius that prove Roman occupation of Exeter 'about the year AD 50'.[51] That is indeed good evidence for the Romans' westward advance, but not for the presence of Vespasian in person, and certainly not for a siege.

In both his accounts, in *Devon and its People* and in *Two Thousand Years in Exeter*, Hoskins leaves the British king and the British queen unnamed, and when we turn to Geoffrey of Monmouth's text, we can see why he was so reticent. The fact is, Geoffrey was much more than just a 'chronicler'; he was one of the great story-tellers of the Middle Ages. His *History of the Kings of Britain*, written (in Latin) about 1130, had an immediate and

[48] R.E.M. Wheeler, *Maiden Castle, Dorset* (Oxford 1943) 61-8.
[49] *Two Thousand Years* (n. 26 above) 7, omitted from the 2004 edition.
[50] *Roman Inscriptions of Britain* 2459.41 (vol. II fasc. 4 [1992] p. 140).
[51] N. Shiel and Richard Reece, in Holbrook and Bidwell (n. 40 above) 24-38.

enormous influence, not least in creating most of the legend of Merlin, Uther Pendragon and King Arthur.

Geoffrey's narrative of the Roman conquest comes in the fourth of his eleven books, and may be summarised as follows.[52]

§ 65 The British king Kimbelinus, a tributary ally of Rome, dies, leaving two sons, Guider and Arviragus. Guider becomes king, and stops paying the tribute. The emperor Claudius invades Britain, landing at Portchester in Kent.

§ 66 Guider and his army engage the Romans, but he is craftily killed by Claudius' general Hamo. Arviragus puts on his brother's armour and leads the Britons to victory. Claudius flees back to the ships, Hamo makes for a different harbour pursued by Arviragus, who kills him there, which is why it's called 'Hamo's port', or South-*ham*pton.

§ 67 Claudius meanwhile has regrouped and pursues Arviragus, besieging him in Winchester. Impressed by the king's defiance, he offers peace and his daughter in marriage if Arviragus will pay the tribute again. Arviragus agrees; Claudius sends to Rome for his daughter, and he and Arviragus go off and conquer the Orkney islands.

§ 68 The emperor's daughter, whose name is Gewissa, arrives and the wedding takes place. At Arviragus' suggestion, Claudius founds a city at the site of the ceremony, and calls it *Glou*-cester after himself. He then returns to Rome, leaving Arviragus in charge of his 'provincial islands'.

§ 69 Arviragus, who has shown himself a successful ruler, once more rejects tributary status, so Claudius sends Vespasian to

---

[52] Geoffrey of Monmouth *Historia regum Britanniae* 65-9 (4.277-361): Michael D. Reeve (ed.), *Geoffrey of Monmouth*, The History of the Kings of Britain (Woodbridge 2007) 80-85.

bring him to order. Prevented by Arviragus' forces from landing in Kent, Vespasian sails down the coast, lands 'on the shore at Totnes', and marches off to besiege Kaerpenhuilgoit, 'which is called Exeter'. Seven days later Arviragus arrives with his army, and there is an inconclusive battle with many casualties. Next day queen Gewissa reconciles the leaders, and Vespasian returns to Rome.

Now, I don't think you can cherry-pick this narrative. It's all of a piece, and if you want the siege you have to take Gewissa with it. Claudius did indeed have a daughter; in fact he had two, Claudia Antonia and Claudia Octavia, both married, as you might expect, to members of the Roman aristocracy.[53] What he did *not* have was a daughter with a Germanic name, married to a Celtic king.

As for Arviragus, he was indeed a British ruler in the first century AD, but we know absolutely nothing about him. His name occurs once in the whole of classical literature, as cited by Geoffrey himself with characteristic effrontery:[54]

Fama igitur per totam Europam diuulgata, diligebant eum Romani et timebant ita ut prae omnibus regibus sermo de eo apud Romam fieret; unde Iuuenalis caecum quendam Neroni dixisse in libro suo commemorat cum de capto rumbo loqueretur inquiens 'regem aliquem capies aut de themone Britanno decidet Aruiragus'.

As Arviragus' fame spread throughout Europe, the Romans respected and feared him to such an extent that he was talked about in Rome beyond all other kings; so Juvenal reports in his book that a certain blind man said to Nero, when talking about

[53] Suetonius *Diuus Claudius* 27.2.
[54] Juvenal 4.126-7; Geoffrey of Monmouth *Historia regum Britanniae* 69 (4.364-8): Reeve (n. 52 above) 86-7.

a newly caught turbot: 'You will capture a king, or Arviragus shall fall from his British chariot-pole.'

In fact it wasn't the blind man who said it, and the emperor he said it to was Domitian, not Nero; but Geoffrey wasn't concerned about doing justice to Juvenal's satire. All he needed was the name of a British king at about the right date, and Juvenal supplied one. Geoffrey himself would supply the events of his reign.

Thanks to Geoffrey, Arviragus had a wonderful afterlife. Chaucer used his name for the noble husband, a Breton knight, in the Franklin's Tale. For the monks of Glastonbury, he was the pagan king who granted Ynyswytrin, 'the Isle of Glass', to Joseph of Arimathea and his followers.[55] From there he got into the great farrago of Holinshed's *Chronicle*, and from there in turn into Shakespeare and Tennyson. Arviragus and his brother are the disguised princes in *Cymbeline* (it is they who sing the great dirge 'Fear no more the heat o' the sun'), and in the *Idylls of the King* the monk Ambrosius tells Sir Percival:[56]

> From our old books I know
> That Joseph came of old to Glastonbury,
> And there the heathen Prince, Arviragus,
> Gave him an isle of marsh whereon to build . . .

And that is exactly where he belongs – in the glorious creative world of pseudo-historical romance that Geoffrey of Monmouth did so much to make possible.

It's easy enough to guess where Geoffrey's siege of Exeter

---

[55] John of Glastonbury *Cronica* 16; James P. Carley (ed.), *The Chronicle of Glastonbury Abbey* (Woodbridge 1985) 38-9, with discussion of the date of the text (c. 1340?) and the origin of the legend at xxv-xxx and xlviii-lx.
[56] 'The Holy Grail', lines 59-62.

came from. In 1066, as in AD 43, a foreign conqueror invaded southern England, and having established his authority there, returned across the Channel. In 1067 Exeter rebelled against William's authority; just so, Geoffrey's Arviragus refused the tribute to Rome. In the winter of 1067–8 William returned, and besieged Exeter; just so, Geoffrey's Claudius sent Vespasian, and he besieged Exeter. Queen Gytha, mother of Harold, was in the city in 1068; so too was Geoffrey's Queen Gewissa in whatever year we are to suppose Vespasian's siege took place. After eighteen days, William's siege ended with generous terms offered to the defenders; after seven days, according to Geoffrey, Vespasian's siege ended the same way.[57] It's obvious, of course: where else would an Anglo-Norman historian look for plausible material to create his narrative?[58]

So when Hoskins, in *Devon and its People* and in *Two Thousand Years in Exeter*, repeatedly described Geoffrey's narrative as 'ancient tradition', was he deliberately misleading his readers? That, I think, is inconceivable. He was a conspicuously honest historian, and he cared deeply about communicating a genuine understanding of the past. No, I think what we have here is a much more interesting phenomenon. Hoskins was persuading his readers to believe Geoffrey's narrative (or at least part of it), because he had already persuaded himself.

---

[57] Geoffrey of Monmouth (n. 52 above) 69; compare Orderic Vitalis *Historia ecclesiastica* 2.179-81 = Marjorie Chibnall (ed.), *The Ecclesiastical History of Orderic Vitalis* vol. 2 (Oxford 1969) 210-15. Gytha: John of Worcester (Florentius Wigoniensis) on 1067 = P. McGurk (ed.), *The Chronicle of John of Worcester* vol. 3 (Oxford 1993) 4-7. Eighteen days: *Anglo-Saxon Chronicle* (MS D) on 1067.

[58] The great siege of Exeter by King Stephen in 1136 may be taken as a *terminus ante quem* for the composition of Geoffrey's fourth book, on the assumption that if he had known about it he would have used it.

5

The Will to Believe

At this point I want to step aside for a moment, and look very briefly, for comparison, at three other cases of 'divining the distant past', namely the Trojan War, Romulus' foundation of Rome, and King Arthur.

Here is another time-chart [Fig. 4], beginning in the second century BC and going back to the Bronze Age palace culture that came to an end, about 1200 BC, with the violent destruction of the palace centres at Knossos, Mycenae and elsewhere. There followed a long period of impoverishment, in which the art of writing was evidently lost, until the Phoenician alphabet was adopted by Greek speakers in the ninth or eighth century.

What matters for our purposes is the composition, probably about 700 BC, of two great epic poems, the *Iliad* and the *Odyssey*, about a great war against Troy conducted by a Greek force under Agamemnon, the king of Mycenae. In their final form they were certainly written down, but it is equally certain that the material they contain was largely created by oral composers, bards celebrating the deeds of men and gods 'to make a song for those who come after'.[59] When Heinrich Schliemann excavated

---

[59] A Homeric formula: *Iliad* 6.357-8, 22.304-5; *Odyssey* 8.579-80.

```
BC/AD
 100    Roman conquest of Greece:  2nd century BC
 200    Timaeus, Eratosthenes:  3rd century BC
 300    Alexander the Great, died 323 BC
 400    Herodotus, writing c. 420 BC
 500
 600  │ Homer:  seventh century BC?
 700  │ First Olympiad, 776 BC
 800  │
 900  │
1000  │
1100  │ "Fall of Troy, 1184 BC"
1200    End of Bronze Age palaces.   Troy VI destroyed c.1270 BC
1300
```

Fig. 4.   Time-chart for Troy

the site of Troy in the 1870s, he was sure he had proved the *Iliad* true. He identified a sequence of layers, of which one, conventionally called 'Troy VI', had evidently been violently destroyed at a date estimated archaeologically at about 1270 BC.

The Greeks believed in the Trojan War as a historical event, and in Homer as a reliable authority. But the Greeks also pioneered rational history, and Herodotus, who was the first to insist on finding out from the evidence rather than just telling stories about the olden days, could guarantee the accuracy of his account only as far back as about 130 years before his own time.[60] I don't think it's coincidence that that is about the same

---

[60] Herodotus 1.5.3 (Croesus of Lydia, c. 550 BC).

space of time allowed by modern anthropologists for the oral transmission of authentic information.[61]

Eventually, research by scholars like Timaeus and Eratosthenes in the Hellenistic period established a reliable dating system, but only as far back as the first Olympiad in 776 BC. Beyond that, all they could do was count generations, in genealogies that might or might not be authentic, and it must have been by that means that Eratosthenes produced a date for the fall of Troy, at what we call 1184 BC.[62] So we have an essentially artificial date that happens to be roughly compatible with the archaeological picture for the end of the Bronze Age.

But the earliest evidence for the Trojan War itself is still Homer, whose poems were put together about five hundred years later. Should we believe his story as the essentially historical record of a Bronze Age conflict? Of course most modern historians say no; but there are still some who follow Schliemann as true believers. Joachim Latacz, for instance, a professor at the University of Basel with a close connection to the ongoing excavations at the site, wrote not long ago an enthusiastic book claiming for Homer the status of 'a source text' for Bronze Age Troy.[63]

Now let's turn to Roman history, and in particular the story of Romulus and Remus and the foundation of the city [Fig. 5]. Our main source is Livy (Titus Livius), writing in the first century BC. He was dependent on previous authors, now lost, of whom the earliest was Fabius Pictor, who wrote the first history

[61] David Henige, 'Impossible to disprove yet impossible to believe: The unforgiving epistemology of deep-time oral tradition', *History in Africa* 36 (2009) 127-234, esp. 201: 'four or five generations seems a generous maximum.'

[62] Eratosthenes (*FGrH* 241 F1) cited by Clement of Alexandria *Stromateis* 1.38.1-3 and Censorinus *De die natali* 21.2-3.

[63] Joachim Latacz, *Troy and Homer: Towards a Solution of an Old Mystery* (trans. K. Windle and R. Ireland, Oxford 2004) 91, 138.

BC/AD	
	Livy: writing c. 20 BC. End of Roman republic
100	Ennius: writing c. 180 BC
200	Fabius Pictor, Naevius: writing c. 210 BC
300	
400	
500	End of Roman monarchy 507 BC
600	
700	"Romulus founds Rome 753 BC"
800	
900	
1000	
1100	"Aeneas escapes from fall of Troy 1184 BC"
1200	

Fig. 5.   Time-chart for Romulus

of Rome about 200 BC. Fabius put Romulus in the eighth century BC,[64] and no doubt he reached that date by counting generations back from the end of the monarchy. However, the foundation story was also told by two early poets, Naevius late in the third century BC and Ennius early in the second; their works too are lost, but we do know that they made Romulus the grandson of Aeneas.[65] Since everyone agreed that Aeneas came to Italy after the fall of Troy, that would put Romulus, and therefore the foundation of Rome, about four hundred years earlier.

None of that mattered for real history until 1988, when Andrea Carandini, excavating on the Palatine, found the remains of a wall, archaeologically dateable to the eighth century BC, on the supposed line of the wall of Romulus' original foundation. He immediately claimed that the Romulus story in Livy was

[64] Rival dates listed in Dionysius of Halicarnassus *Roman Antiquities* 1.74.1-3 and Solinus *Collectanea rerum memorabilius* 1.27-30.
[65] Servius *auctus* on Virgil *Aeneid* 1.273.

thus proved to be historical; indeed, he had found the very wall that Remus had contemptuously jumped over in the story of the twins.[66] There's no point asking why he privileges the Livian version of the foundation story rather than that of Naevius and Ennius, which would put it in the late Bronze Age; it's obviously because only the Livian version matches the date of his wall.

Most people regard this as sheer fantasy; but Carandini is the most prominent archaeologist in Italy – 'the Lord of the Digs', as *La Stampa* called him – and he expects what he says to be taken seriously.[67] His vision of early Rome is now enshrined in the standard work on the ancient topography of the city, the magnificent *Atlas of Ancient Rome*.[68] Here too we have a true believer, and a very influential one.

In both these cases a legendary event is claimed as historical, and the distance between its supposed date and the earliest evidence for it is about five hundred years. In my third example, King Arthur, it's nearly six hundred [Fig. 6], from Geoffrey of Monmouth, who first told the story, back to the date Geoffrey gave for the king's death. You could, I suppose, call it three hundred years, from the first datable mention of Arthur – as a legendary war-leader (*dux bellorum*), not a king – in the ninth-century *Historia Brittonum*.[69] But even that is well beyond Herodotus' 130-year limit for reliable tradition.

Now of course there is no shortage of true believers in King Arthur, but serious scholars are not among them. However, one distinguished historian, Ronald Hutton, finds that regrettable: at the end of his brilliant essay on 'Arthur and the academics', he

[66] Convenient English summary in Andrea Carandini, *Rome: Day One* (Princeton 2011).
[67] 'Il Signore degli Scavi', *La Stampa* 14 Feb. 2009 ('Tuttolibri' p. xi).
[68] Andrea Carandini (ed.), *Atlante di Roma Antica* (Milan 2012). See the review in *Journal of Roman Studies* 103 (2013) 234-68.
[69] 'Nennius' *Historia Brittonum* 56, 73.

1100	Geoffrey of Monmouth c. 1130
1000	
900	
800	'Nennius' *Historia Brittonum* c. 830
700	
600	
500	"Death of Arthur 542"
400	Last (western) Roman emperor 476
300	Constantinople founded 324
200	
100	
AD/BC	Roman conquest of Britain 43

Fig. 6. Time-chart for Arthur

confesses to the uneasy feeling that 'the current tendency among specialists to write off Arthur altogether . . . begs the enormous question of how a character who may never have existed came, within three hundred years of his presumed lifetime, to be the greatest hero of his people'.[70] One suspects that despite his cool assessment of the evidence, Professor Hutton would *like* to be a true believer.

What these three cases have in common was identified long ago by Moses Finley in his classic article on the Trojan War: he called it 'the will to believe'.[71] If you *want* to believe in something strongly enough, you may find it easy to overlook the arguments against it.

I think that's what happened when Hoskins came to live in Exeter in 1955. Previously, he had known very well, and stated in print, that there is no good reason to believe in a pre-Roman

[70] Ronald Hutton, *Witches, Druids and King Arthur* (London and New York 2003) 58.
[71] M.I. Finley, 'The Trojan War', *Journal of Hellenic Studies* 84 (1964) 2.

settlement at Exeter; but once he started work on the history of the city, he evidently convinced himself otherwise. The interesting question is *why* he should have done that.

We may find an answer if we remember the book Hoskins is most famous for, *The Making of the English Landscape*, published in 1955. It was never meant as a definitive account, and his ideas on the subject did not remain static. That was a point he emphasised in the book he wrote eighteen years later to accompany the first of his television programmes. He was glad now, he said, of the opportunity 'to air a few new ideas' – and one of them was 'the powerful imprint made upon the landscape' in the prehistoric and Roman periods, something he had 'dismissed too briefly' in the original book.[72] And that led him to announce a general principle, one that he repeated in all subsequent editions of *The Making of the English Landscape*. It was stated in epigrammatic form and emphatic italics: *'Everything is older than we think'*.[73]

Hoskins came to live in Exeter in the year his first landscape book was published. It is as certain as such things can be that when he set about his project for a full-scale history of the city, he began by thinking about the site, the landscape which was there before the city existed. He looked at Polsloe Road and Sidwell Street, and saw that they could have been ancient ridgeway routes; he looked at the old Bartholomew Yard cemetery, and saw that it could have been an Iron Age promontory fort. 'Everything is older than we think' – but he needed a reason to move from 'could have been' to 'must have been'.

---

[72] WGH, *English Landscapes* (London 1973) 6.
[73] *English Landscapes* (n. 72 above) 6; one of the 'leading ideas' that were 'becoming more and more impressed on my mind'. Repeated (again in italics) in the Introduction to the 1977 edition of *The Making of the English Landscape*, and all others thereafter. See also WGH, *One Man's England* (London 1978) 12: 'Everything is more ancient than it looks'.

That reason was provided by Captain Shortt's coins, which would not be definitively disqualified as historical evidence for another thirty years. If they really implied a pre-Roman trading centre, then why not believe in Vespasian's siege of Exeter in Geoffrey of Monmouth? Hoskins *wanted* to believe it, and so he convinced himself that that bit of Geoffrey's narrative was not historical fiction invented in 1130 but the record of a real event somehow transmitted from a thousand years before.

We began this little book with Hoskins at Honeychurch, trying to think himself back into the past and running up against a barrier beyond which he knew it couldn't be done. I think that was a brave and honest thing for a historian to say. There is always a temptation to outrun the evidence, to treat distant and unattested eras as if they were as intelligible as periods documented by written records. Hoskins was too good a historian to succumb to that temptation – except when it came to dealing with the origins of his native city.

Coming to live there clearly made a difference. In his book on local history, written at just that time, Hoskins used a couple of lines of Horace as an epigraph: *ille terrarum mihi praeter omnes | angulus ridet*, 'It is that corner of the world above all that has a smile for me'.[74] Half a century later his book on Exeter is still in print, now splendidly illustrated and up-dated,[75] and the coins, the Mediterranean trade, the 'ancient tradition'

[74] WGH, *Local History in England* (London 1959) iii; Horace *Odes* 2.6.13-14 (on Tibur).
[75] Hazel Harvey in WGH, *Two Thousand Years in Exeter* (Chichester 2004) x: 'Some information included in the first edition has now been omitted or modified in the light of later developments, but generally I have been reluctant to make changes to Hoskins' authoritative text.'

and Vespasian's siege are all still there, having survived the demolition of the evidence they were based on. They are there thanks to historical fiction in the twelfth century, a historical hoax in the nineteenth, and the extraordinary power of the 'will to believe'.

This text originated as the thirtieth in the series of Jackson Knight Memorial Lectures in the University of Exeter (3 October 2014).

W. F. Jackson Knight (1895–1964), Virgilian scholar and spiritualist, taught in the Exeter Classics Department from 1935 to 1961. His Penguin translation of the *Aeneid* sold about half a million copies and stayed in print for over forty years. He was a wonderfully inspiring teacher, and when he died the Jackson Knight Memorial Lecture fund was raised jointly by the students in the Department and by his friends and colleagues, to perpetuate the memory of his work and ideas, and to establish lectures 'on topics connected with Latin and Greek literature, its influences on modern literature, classical anthropology, and ancient thought in all its aspects', to be given by persons 'who have achieved distinction in academic or literary work or in public life'. As the founders intended, over the last fifty years the Jackson Knight Lecturers have included not only classical scholars but also poets, novelists, critics, historians and other distinguished figures, including a Poet Laureate (Cecil Day Lewis, 1969) and an Oscar winner (Frederic Raphael, 2011).

Index